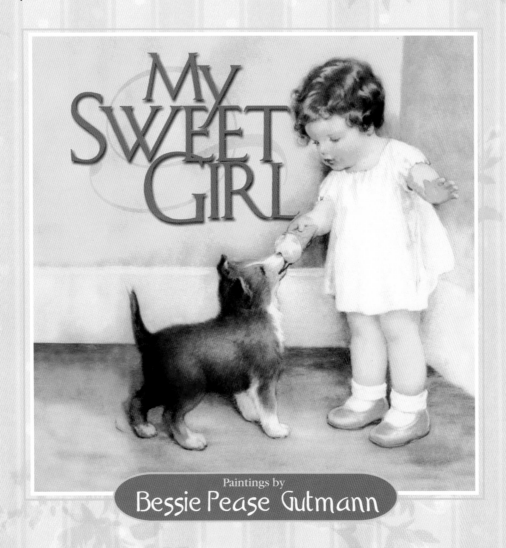

My Sweet Girl

Paintings by
Bessie Pease Gutmann

HARVEST HOUSE PUBLISHERS

EUGENE, OREGON

My Sweet Girl

Text Copyright © 2005 by Harvest House Publishers
Eugene, Oregon 97402

ISBN 0-7369-1516-8

Printed in China.

05 06 07 08 09 10 11 / IM / 7 6 5 4 3 2 1.

Who ever would think that so much went on in the soul of a young girl?

ANNE FRANK

Tom had often caught glimpses of this little girl,—for she was one of those busy, tripping creatures, that can be no more contained in one place than a sunbeam or a summer breeze,—nor was she one that, once seen, could be easily forgotten. Her form was the perfection of childish beauty...An airy and innocent playfulness seemed to flicker like the shadow of summer leaves over her childish face, and around her buoyant figure. She was always in motion, always with a half smile on her rosy mouth, flying hither and thither, with an undulating and cloudlike tread, singing to herself as she moved as in a happy dream.

HARRIET BEECHER STOWE
Uncle Tom's Cabin

Every child is an artist.
PABLO PICASSO

There was a little girl

Who had a little curl

Right in the middle of her forehead;

And when she was good

She was very, very good,

But when she was bad she was horrid.

HENRY WADSWORTH LONGFELLOW

Little girls *are the nicest things that happen to people. They are*

born with a little bit of angelshine about them, and though it wears

thin sometimes there is always enough left to lasso your heart--even

when they are sitting in the mud, or crying temperamental tears, or

parading up the street in mother's best clothes.

ALAN BECK

Allow children to be happy in their own way, for what better way will they find?

DR. SAMUEL JOHNSON

In her blue dress, with her cheeks lightly

flushed, her blue, blue eyes, and her gold

curls pinned up as though for the first time

. . . Mrs. Raddick's daughter might have

just dropped from this radiant heaven.

KATHERINE MANSFIELD
THE YOUNG GIRL

Every little girl knows about love.

Dr. Samuel Johnson

Amy is like the lark she writes about, trying to get up among

the clouds, but always dropping down into its nest again. Dear little girl!

She's so ambitious, but her heart is good and tender, and no matter how

high she flies, she never will forget home.

LOUSIA MAY ALCOTT
Little Women

What a charming little girl she was! Pale, fragile, light—
she looked as though a breath would send her flying like
a feather to the skies…

ANTON CHEKHOV
Lights

The greatest poem ever known

Is one all poets have outgrown:

The poetry, innate, untold,

Of being only four years old.

CHRISTOPHER MORLEY
"To a Child"

Daddy dear, I'm only four
And I'd rather not be more:
Four's the nicest age to be—
Two and two, or one and three.

All I love is two and two,
Mother, Fabian, Paul and you;
All you love is one and three,
Mother, Fabian, Paul and me.
Give your little girl a kiss
Because she learned and told you this.

EDITH NESBIT
The Rainbow and the Rose

A child is fed with milk and praise.

MARY LAMB

My Little Girl

A weary little mortal
Has gone to slumberland;
The Pixies at the portal
Have caught her by the hand.
She dreams her broken dolly
Will soon be mended there,
That looks so melancholy
Upon the rocking-chair.

My little girl is nested
Within her tiny bed,
With amber ringlets crested
Around her dainty head;
She lies so calm and stilly,
She breathes so soft and low,
She calls to mind a lily
Half-hidden in the snow.

I kiss your wayward tresses,
My drowsy little queen;
I know you have caresses
From floating forms unseen.
O, Angels, let me keep her
To kiss away my cares,
This darling little sleeper,
Who has my love and prayers!

SAMUEL MINTURN PECK

"What I believe about dolls," *she said,*

"is that they can do things they will not let us know about. Perhaps, really, Emily can read and talk and walk, but she will only do it when people are out of the room. That is her secret. You see, if people knew that dolls could do things, they would make them work. So, perhaps, they have promised each other to keep it a secret. If you stay in the room, Emily will just sit there and stare; but if you go out, she will begin to read, perhaps, or go and look out of the window. Then if she heard either of us coming, she would just run back and jump into her chair and pretend she had been there all the time."

FRANCIS HODGSON BURNETT
A Little Princess

"Her eyes were a burning blue, the lashes curled like a doll's lashes, and the brows as even and dark as a doll's, too."

KATHLEEN THOMPSON NORRIS
Austin's Girl

The sunlight through an oriel window

fell on the childish face and figure,

glinting the yellow hair, and lighting

up the radiant face, that yet had a

tender, loving glance. . .

Margaret Sidney
FIVE LITTLE PEPPERS AND HOW THEY GREW

I think, at a child's birth, if a mother could ask a fairy godmother to endow it with the most useful gift, that gift should be curiosity.
ELEANOR ROOSEVELT

Praise the young and they will blossom.

Irish Proverb

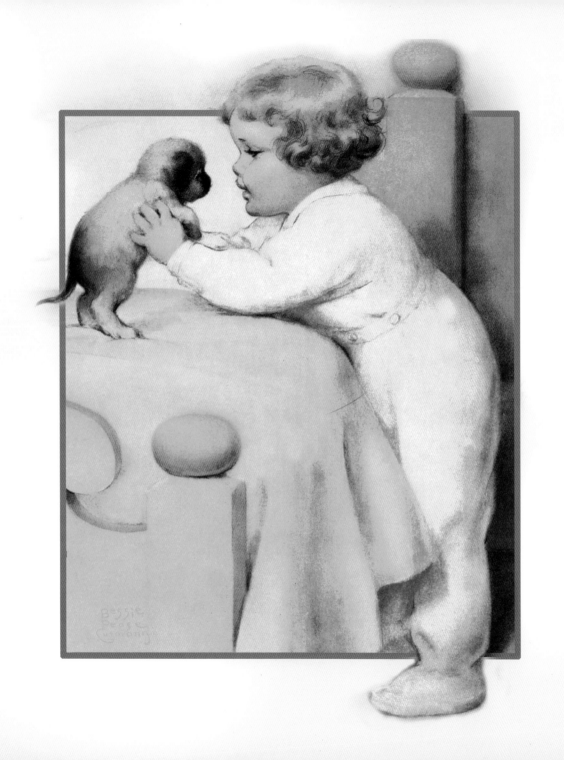

Her face was fair and
pretty, with eyes like
two bits of night sky,
each with a star
dissolved in the blue.
Those eyes you would
have thought must have
known they came from
there, so often were
they turned up in
that direction.

GEORGE MACDONALD
The Princess and the Goblin

"Don't she look sweet, the dear!"

murmured Mrs. Moss, proudly surveying her

youngest. She certainly did. . .It was no

wonder mother and sister thought there never

was such a perfect child as "our Betty."

LOUISA MAY ALCOTT
Under the Lilacs

Her frank, clear eyes bespeak a mind
Old-world traditions fail to bind.
    She is not shy
Or bold, but simply self-possessed;
Her independence adds a zest
Unto her speech, her piquant jest,
    Her quaint reply.

ETHEL CASTILLA

"I do *not* like patchwork," said Anne dolefully, hunting out her workbasket and sitting down before a little heap of red and white diamonds with a sigh. "I think some kinds of sewing would be nice; but there's no scope for imagination in patchwork. It's just one little seam after another and you never seem to be getting anywhere. But of course I'd rather be Anne of Green Gables sewing patchwork than Anne of any other place with nothing to do but play."

L.M. MONTGOMERY
Anne of Green Gables

The dull day brightened

wonderfully after that, and the time flew pleasantly, as tongues and needles went together. Grandma peeped in, and smiled at the busy group, saying, "Sew away, my dears; dollies are safe companions, and needlework an accomplishment that's sadly neglected nowadays. Small stitches, Maud; neat buttonholes, Fan; cut carefully, Polly, and don't waste your cloth. Take pains; and the best needlewoman shall have a pretty bit of white satin for a doll's bonnet."

LOUISA MAY ALCOTT
An Old-Fashioned Girl

They had a little girl with

fair curls, who wore a

gold locket and was

dressed like a princess.

EDITH WHARTON

Of all nature's gifts to

the human race, what is

sweeter to a man than

his children?

MARCUS TULLIUS CICERO

Children are a poor man's riches.

ENGLISH PROVERB

A grandfather was walking through his yard

when he heard his granddaugther repeating the

alphabet in a tone of voice that sounded like a

prayer. He asked her what she was doing. The

little girl explained: "I'm praying, but I can't

think of exactly the right words, so I'm just saying

all the letters, and God will put them together

for me, because He knows what I'm thinking."

CHARLES B. VAUGHAN

The best and most beautiful things
in the world cannot be seen, nor
touched...but are felt in the heart.

Helen Keller

Daddy's Little Girl

AUTHOR UNKNOWN

You're the end of the rainbow,
My pot of gold;
You're Daddy's little girl
To have and hold.
A precious gem
Is what you are;
You're Mommy's
Bright and shining star.

You're the spirit of Christmas,
My star on the tree;
You're the Easter bunny
To Mommy and me.
You're sugar you're spice,
You're everything nice;
And you're
Daddy's little girl.

You're the end of the rainbow,
My pot of gold;
You're Daddy's little girl
To have and hold.
A precious gem
Is what you are;
You're Mommy's
Bright and shining star.

You're the treasure I cherish
So sparkling and bright;
You were touched by the holy
And beautiful light.
Like angels that sing,
A heavenly thing,
And you're
Daddy's little girl.

Cradle Song

Sleep, sleep, beauty bright,

Dreaming in the joys of night;

Sleep, sleep; in thy sleep

Little sorrows sit and weep.

Sweet babe, in thy face

Soft desires I can trace,

Secret joys and secret smiles,

Little pretty infant wiles.

WILLIAM BLAKE

Hush, my dear, lie still and slumber

Holy Angels guard thy bed!

Heavenly blessings without number

Gently falling on thy head.

Isaac Watts

My little girl dressed up in flowers and bows—

time passes too quickly a wise mother knows.

So I'll cherish the giggles I hear on this day—

along with each smile she sends my way.

Tami Potter